MW01172541

PRE-MED TRACK

FOR 1ST GRADERS

ANATOMY & PHYSIOLOGY:

SKELETAL SYSTEM

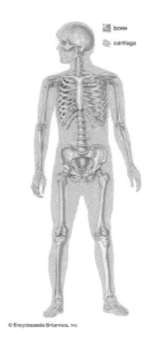

bone

cartilage

© Encyclopædia Britannica, Inc.

REAPING TIME OUTREACH WORSHIP CENTER

WRITTEN BY DR. TASHA TAYLOR

Introduction to Missions Students of:

"You Tread Christian Academy Virtual School," and "Tasha Taylor's Christian School, High School and Seminary in Pakistan" God bless your dedication, endeavor to carry your cross for Jesus, and love for Jesus around the World. I love you dearly and Ye Shall Tread in every area of your lives!!

TABLE OF CONTENTS

Pre- Med Track

1st Graders Anatomy Book

Chapter 1- Lesson 1 "Skeletal System"

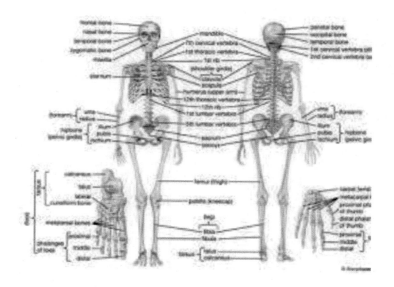

Anatomy - The Skeletal System

Ms. Sylvia- Nurse (a volunteer nurse)

Anatomy is the study of the body structure. The cells influence the body structure. Cells are what makes our bodies work like nucleus, cytoplasm and cell membrane. Cells contain genetic materials. Things needed in the body are what makes the body and organs work. The organs in our bodies work with our cells. Mitosis is the process of the reproductive system. When cells divide it is called mitosis. Cells give us nutrients and energy. Cytoplasm is the process of breaking down cells. Energy and temperature is eliminated through waste through cells in the body. Connective tissues provide support and cells are part of the body.

Epithelial tissues

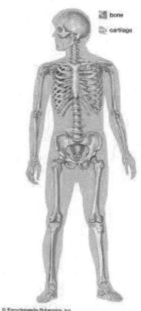

bone

cartilage

© Encyclopædia Britannica, Inc.

cover the body both inside and outside of the body. The body tissues that contract are our muscle tissue. Tissues that make legs and bones move are muscle cells. Organs are brain, heart, lungs, eyes and skin tissues. Largest organ of the human body is the skin. The endocrine system controls hormones growth and development. Skin protects, covers and regulates body temperature. Skin covers the body parts as well. Healthy ways of losing weight are through exercise. Brain cells and the nervous system are not replaceable unless there is a miracle.

The Skeletal System

Use the given word bank to name the indicated parts of the skeletal system.

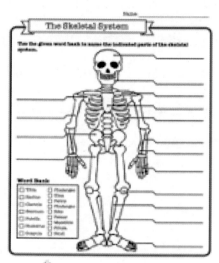

Word Bank

- ☐ Tibia
- ☐ Carina
- ☐ Clavicle
- ☐ Sternum
- ☐ Patella
- ☐ Humerus
- ☐ Scapula
- ☐ Phalanges
- ☐ Ulna
- ☐ Pelvis
- ☐ Phalanges
- ☐ Ribs
- ☐ Femur
- ☐ Mandible
- ☐ Fibula
- ☐ Skull

محترمہ سلویا۔ نرس (ایک رضاکار نرس)

اناٹومی جسمانی ساخت کا مطالعہ ہے۔ خلیات جسم کی ساخت کو متاثر کرتے ہیں۔ خلیات وہ ہیں جو ہمارے جسم کو نیوکلئس، سائٹوپلازم اور سیل جھلی کی طرح کام کرتے ہیں۔ خلیوں میں جینیاتی مواد ہوتا ہے۔ جسم میں ضروری چیزیں وہی ہیں جو جسم اور اعضاء کو کام کرتی ہیں۔ ہمارے جسم کے اعضاء ہمارے خلیات کے ساتھ کام کرتے ہیں۔ مائٹوسس تولیدی نظام کا عمل ہے۔ جب خلیات تقسیم ہوتے ہیں تو اسے مائٹوسس کہتے ہیں۔ خلیے ہمیں غذائی اجزاء اور توانائی دیتے ہیں۔

سائٹوپلازم خلیوں کو توڑنے کا عمل ہے۔ جسم میں خلیات کے ذریعے فضلہ کے ذریعے توانائی اور درجہ حرارت کا خاتمہ ہوتا ہے۔ کنیکٹیو ٹشوز مدد فراہم کرتے ہیں اور خلیات جسم کا حصہ ہیں۔ ایپیٹیلیل ٹشوز جسم کو جسم کے اندر اور باہر دونوں طرح سے ڈھانپتے ہیں۔ جسم کے ٹشوز جو سکڑتے ہیں وہ ہمارے پٹھوں کے ٹشو ہیں۔ ٹانگوں اور ہڈیوں کو حرکت دینے والے ٹشوز پٹھوں کے خلیات ہیں۔ اعضاء دماغ، دل، پھیپھڑے، آنکھیں اور جلد کے ٹشوز ہیں۔

انسانی جسم کا سب سے بڑا عضو جلد ہے۔ اینڈوکرائن سسٹم ہارمونز کی نشوونما اور نشوونما کو کنٹرول کرتا ہے۔ جلد جسم کے درجہ حرارت کی حفاظت، احاطہ اور کنٹرول کرتی ہے۔ جلد جسم کے حصوں کو بھی ڈھانپتی ہے۔

وزن کم کرنے کے صحت مند طریقے ورزش کے ذریعے ہیں۔ دماغی خلیات
اور اعصابی نظام تبدیل نہیں ہوسکتے جب تک کہ کوئی معجزہ نہ ہو۔

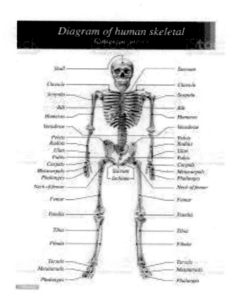

Review our Skeletal Anatomy

Vertebrae- in the back of the body the different

bones in the body. This bone goes down the back

to the coxal bone.

Sternum- in the front of the body and below the clavicle. The Femur is the upper bone in the leg.

ہماری اسکیلیٹل اناٹومی کا جائزہ لیں۔

ورٹیبرا ۔ جسم کے پچھلے حصے میں جسم میں مختلف ہڈیاں۔ یہ ہڈی پیچھے سے نیچے کوکسل ہڈی تک جاتی ہے۔

Sternum- جسم کے سامنے اور ہنسلی کے نیچے۔ فیمر ٹانگ میں اوپری ہڈی ہے۔

The longest bone in the human body is the femur. The Humerus - is the upper bone in the arm. The Cranium covers our brain. The Scientific name for our wrist are carpals. Our Metacarpals are in between fingers and wrist are the Metacarpals Phalanges are the scientific name for fingers and toes. Our Arms have two bones in the lower arm called the radial and the ulnar. The ulnar is under the radius. Remember under for ulnar. Patella - the kneecap is called Patella

بازو میں اوپری - **Humerus** انسانی جسم کی سب سے لمبی ہڈی فیمر ہے۔

ہڈی ہے۔ کرینیم ہمارے دماغ کا احاطہ کرتا ہے۔ ہماری کلائی کا سائنسی نام

انگلیوں کے درمیان ہیں اور کلائی **Metacarpals** کارپل ہے۔ ہمارے

Metacarpals ہیں۔

انگلیوں اور انگلیوں کا سائنسی نام ہے۔ ہمارے بازووں کے **Phalanges**

نچلے بازو میں دو ہڈیاں ہوتی ہیں جنہیں ریڈیل اور النار کہتے ہیں۔ النار رداس

کے نیچے ہے۔ النر کے لیے یاد رکھیں۔

پٹیلا - گھٹنے کی ٹوپی کو پٹیلہ کہتے ہیں۔

Under the kneecap tarsals (ankle) metatarsals
are in-between tarsals and phalanges. There
are206 bones in the human body. Another name
for tibia is the shin bone. The lower leg has two
bones called the tibia and fibula. Also, the
Pelvis- has the pubis bones ilium, ischium and
pubis are 3 of them.

گھٹنے کیپ ٹارسل (ٹخنوں) کے نیچے میٹاٹرسل ٹارسل اور فالنگس کے درمیان

ہوتے ہیں۔ انسانی جسم میں 206 ہڈیاں ہوتی ہیں۔ ٹبیا کا دوسرا نام پنڈلی کی

ہڈی ہے۔ نچلی ٹانگ میں دو ہڈیاں ہوتی ہیں جنہیں ٹبیا اور فیبولا کہتے ہیں۔ اس

کے علاوہ، شرونی میں پیبس کی ہڈیاں ilium ،ischium اور pubis

ہوتی ہیں ان میں سے 3 ہیں۔

Ms. Elise -Nurse

Our teeth are bones and food, drinks and sugar takes the enamel off of our teeth. The enamel protects our teeth naturally built from the body. The breaking down of the enamel causes plaque to develop which are dead white and red blood cells on the teeth.

ہمارے دانت ہڈیاں ہیں اور کھانا، مشروبات اور چینی ہمارے دانتوں کے تامچینی

کو اتار دیتے ہیں۔ انامیل ہمارے دانتوں کی حفاظت کرتا ہے جو قدرتی طور پر

جسم سے بنے ہیں۔ تامچینی کے ٹوٹنے سے تختی بنتی ہے جو دانتوں پر مردہ سفید اور سرخ خون کے خلیات ہوتے ہیں۔

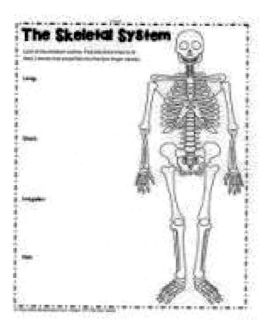

The Skeletal System

Another word for our kneecap is called Patella. The Longest bone in the human body is called the Femur and it accounts for one-third of a human's height. Our Femur is found between the hip joint and the patella. The tibia and fibula are the two bones in the lower leg; the fibula is more distal and the tibia is in the front. The humerus

is bone in the upper arm. The lower leg, at the

ankle bone is called the tarsal. In between our

tarsal and toes are the metatarsals.

Bone in the hands and the feet comprise half of

all the bones in the human body. There are 106

bones in hands and the feet. Our wrist is called

the carpal and the area between wrist and

forehand is the metacarpal. Our fingers are

called phalanges and our toes are termed the same scientific name, phalanges.

The skeleton is the body's framework. The skeleton protects the body, brains and the heart and the lungs. The skeletal system is divided into the Axial and Appendicular skeleton. The costae are formed with 24 ribs

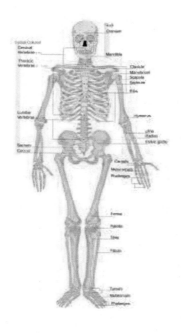

کنکال نظام

ہمارے گھٹنے کیپ کے لیے ایک اور لفظ پٹیلہ کہلاتا ہے۔ انسانی جسم کی سب سے لمبی ہڈی کو فیمر کہا جاتا ہے اور یہ انسانی قد کا ایک تہائی حصہ بنتی ہے۔ ہمارا فیمر کولہے کے جوڑ اور پیٹیلا کے درمیان پایا جاتا ہے۔ ٹبیا اور فیبولا نچلی ٹانگ میں دو ہڈیاں ہیں۔ فبولا زیادہ دور ہے اور ٹبیا سامنے ہے۔ humerus اوپری بازو میں ہڈی ہے۔ ٹخنے کی ہڈی پر نچلی ٹانگ کو ترسل کہتے ہیں۔ ہمارے ٹارسل اور انگلیوں کے درمیان میٹاٹرسلز ہیں۔

ہاتھ اور پاؤں کی ہڈی انسانی جسم کی تمام ہڈیوں کا نصف پر مشتمل ہوتی ہے۔

ہاتھوں اور پیروں میں **106** ہڈیاں ہیں۔ ہماری کلائی کو کارپل کہا جاتا ہے اور

کلائی اور پیشانی کے درمیان کا حصہ میٹا کارپل ہے۔ ہماری انگلیوں کو

phalanges کہا جاتا ہے اور ہماری انگلیوں کو اسی سائنسی نام،

phalanges کہا جاتا ہے۔

کنکال جسم کا فریم ورک ہے۔ کنکال جسم، دماغ اور دل اور پھیپھڑوں کی

حفاظت کرتا ہے۔ کنکال کے نظام کو محوری اور اپینڈیکولر کنکال میں تقسیم کیا

گیا ہے۔ کوسٹے **24** پسلیوں سے بنتے ہیں۔

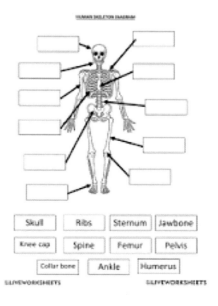

The bones of the Skull: occipital, sphenoid bone, ethmoid, temporal bone, lacrimal, frontal, lacrimal bone, zygomatic bone, parietal and the ethmoid bone. Temporal bones found at the sides of the head and skull.

Facial bones- Maxilla, mandible (jaw bone) is the largest bone in the face and the only movable bone in the skull, palatine, vomer forms the inferior part of the nasal septum, works together with the sphenoid, ethmoid, palatine bones and maxillary bones. The Nasal conchae, the nasal bone and bones of the ear are the smallest bones in the body hammer, anvil and stirrup aka malleolus, incus and stapes.

Vertebrae- in the back of the body the different bones in the body. This bone goes down the back to the coxal bone. Sternum- in the front of the body and below the clavicle. Femur- upper bone in the leg. The longest bone in the human body is the femur. Humerus - is the long bone in our arm and distal to this bone is our "funny bone." Cranium - covers our brain. Our wrist are

Can you draw this figure and label it with scientific names?

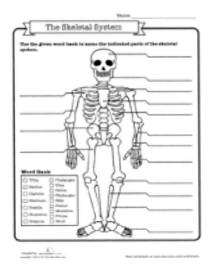

Can you say the scientific names 5x each

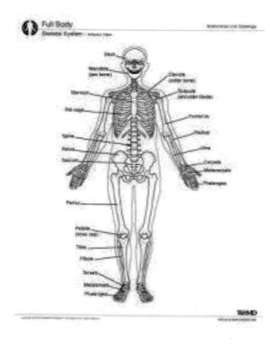

called carpals. Our metacarpals are - in-between fingers and wrist. Our phalanges are the scientific name given for our fingers and toes. The lower arm has two bones known as the radius and the Ulna is for under the wrist.

occipital, sphenoid bone, ethmoid, :کھوپڑی کی ہڈیاں temporal bone, lacrimal, frontal, lacrimal bone, zygomatic bone, parietal and the ethmoid bone.

سر اور کھوپڑی کے اطراف میں پائی جانے والی عارضی ہڈیاں۔ چہرے کی ہڈیاں۔ میکسلا، مینڈیبل (جبڑے کی ہڈی) چہرے کی سب سے بڑی ہڈی ہے اور کھوپڑی میں واحد حرکت پذیر ہڈی ہے، پیلیٹائن، وومر ناک کے پردہ کا کمتر حصہ بناتی ہے، اسفینائیڈ، ایتھمائڈ، پیلیٹائن ہڈیوں اور میکسیلری کے ساتھ مل کر کام کرتی ہے۔ ہڈیوں۔ ناک کی ہڈی، ناک کی ہڈی اور کان کی ہڈیاں جسم کے ہتھوڑے، اینول اور رکاب عرف میلیولس، انکس اور سٹیپس کی سب سے چھوٹی ہڈیاں ہیں۔

ورٹیبرا ۔ جسم کے پچھلے حصے میں جسم میں مختلف ہڈیاں۔ یہ ہڈی پیچھے

سے نیچے کوکسل ہڈی تک جاتی ہے۔ -Sternum جسم کے سامنے اور

ہنسلی کے نیچے۔ فیمر ۔ ٹانگ میں اوپری ہڈی۔ انسانی جسم کی سب سے لمبی

ہڈی فیمر ہے۔ ہیومرس ۔ ہمارے بازو کی لمبی ہڈی ہے اور اس ہڈی سے دور

ہماری "مضحکہ خیز ہڈی" ہے۔ کرینیم ۔ ہمارے دماغ کا احاطہ کرتا ہے۔ ہماری

کلائی کو کارپل کہتے ہیں۔ ہمارے میٹا کارپل ہیں ۔ انگلیوں اور کلائی کے

درمیان۔ ہمارے phalanges ہماری انگلیوں اور انگلیوں کے لیے دیا جانے

والا سائنسی نام ہے۔ نچلے بازو میں دو ہڈیاں ہیں جنہیں رداس کہا جاتا ہے اور

النا کلائی کے نیچے کے لیے ہے۔

Can you label the bones 1-19?

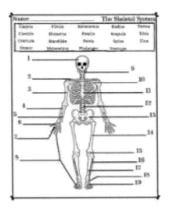

1.

2.

3.

4.

5.

6.

7.

8.

9.

10.

11.

12.

13.

14.

15.

16.

16.

17.

18.

19.

Draw, Color and label each bone with its

scientific name, on the next page.

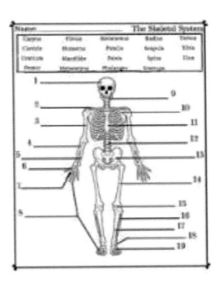

Draw the picture here.

Lets Review

1. The Kneecap is called

   the_____

2. What are the tarsals?

3. What are the metatarsals?

4. What is in between, tarsals and phalanges?

5. What bones are in between the tarsals and

   the phalanges?

6. The shin bone is what body part? (hint

   rhymes with fibula)

Short bones are the seven tarsals. Pelvis- has

the pubis bones ilium, ischium and pubis are 3 of

them.

آئیے جائزہ لیں۔

گھٹنے کیپ کو ـــــــــــــــــــــــــــــــــــ کہا جاتا ہے

tarsals کیا ہیں؟

metatarsals کیا ہیں؟

tarsals اور phalanges کے درمیان کیا ہے؟

tarsals اور phalanges کے درمیان کون سی ہڈیاں ہیں؟

پنڈلی کی ہڈی جسم کا کون سا حصہ ہے؟ (فبلا کے ساتھ اشارے والی نظمیں)

چھوٹی ہڈیاں، سات ترسل ہیں۔ Pelvis- میں pubis ہڈیوں، ilium

ischium اور pubis ان میں سے 3 ہیں۔

Prepare for your Anatomy test! Label the skeleton with its scientific bone names.

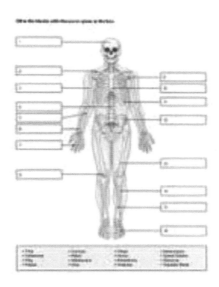

Chapter II: Lesson 2

Anatomy: The Brain

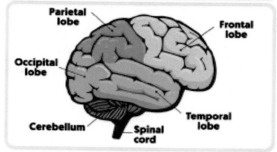

PARTS OF THE BRAIN

Parietal lobe

Frontal lobe

Occipital lobe

Temporal lobe

Cerebellum

Spinal cord

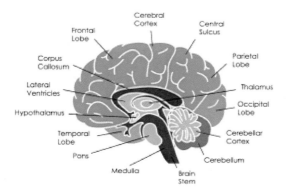

Anatomy: The Brain

- **The skeletal system is what helps our bodies have form and walk properly. Among its many functions the skeletal system protects all vital organs, such as: the heart, liver, kidneys, etc... The skeletal system can be divided into two**

sections, the axial and the appendicular

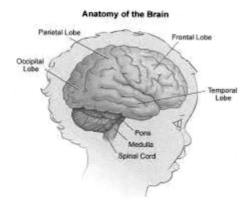

Anatomy of the Brain

- **skeleton. In the axial skeleton this comprises our ribs and our spine. The stardom is also known as the breast bone. The skull has 8 different pegs. The brain pegs will be listed here. Our Volunteer Nurse Ms. Louise explained them to be called our Cranals, which are:**
  - **Olfactory- a malfunction of this peg would cause a problem with hearing**

or smelling.

Parts of the Human Brain

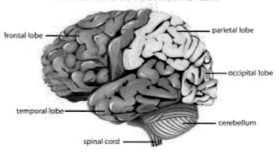

- o **Optic- a malfunction of the optic nerve would result in myopia and glaucoma**
- o **Oculomotor- deals with the movement of the eyelids.**
- o **Troclar- this peg works with the muscle of the eye.**

Human Brain Anatomy

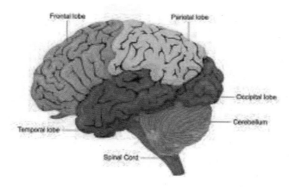

- o **Trigeminal nerve brain peg malfunction causes difficulty chewing and muscle reflex.**
- o **Abducens- movement of the eye**
- o **Facial brain pegs- concerns movement of the face and decreases facial secretions and a person can not feel facial sensation.**

o   **Vestibulocochlear or acoustic nerve-
malfunction of brain peg would lead
to loss of balance or movement**

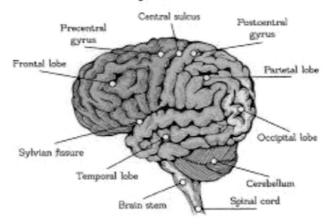

Anatomy of the brain

o   **Glossopharyngeal- malfunction of
this brain peg would lead to difficulty
swallowing and getting salvia
because aspiration is needed for
swallowing.**

- o **Vagus Loube- this nerve deals with phobia, speech, respiratory, digestive and reflex.**
- o **Final accessory- is a brain peg**
- o **Hypoglossal- is another brain peg.**

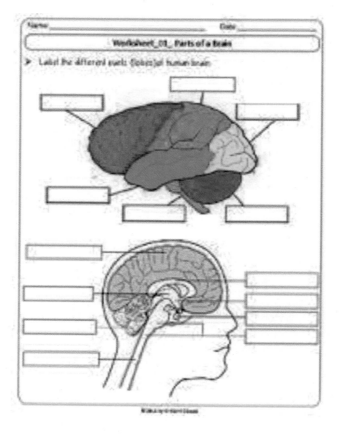

Label the parts of the human Brain.

کنکال نظام

• کنکال کا نظام وہ ہے جو ہمارے جسموں کو صحیح شکل میں چلنے اور چلنے میں مدد کرتا ہے۔ اس کے بہت سے کاموں میں سے کنکال نظام تمام اہم اعضاء کی حفاظت کرتا ہے، جیسے: دل، جگر، گردے، وغیرہ... کنکال کے نظام کو دو حصوں میں تقسیم کیا جا سکتا ہے، محوری اور اپینڈیکولر کنکال۔ محوری کنکال میں یہ ہماری پسلیاں اور ہماری ریڑھ کی ہڈی پر مشتمل ہوتا ہے۔ سٹارنڈم کو چھاتی کی ہڈی بھی کہا جاتا ہے۔ کھوپڑی میں 8 مختلف کھونٹے ہوتے ہیں۔ دماغ کے کھونٹے یہاں درج کیے جائیں گے۔ ہماری رضاکار نرس محترمہ لوئیس نے انہیں ہمارے کرینلز کہلانے کی وضاحت کی، جو یہ ہیں:

o- Olfactory اس پیگ کی خرابی سے سننے یا سونگھنے میں دشواری ہوگی۔

o آپٹک- آپٹک اعصاب کی خرابی کے نتیجے میں میوپیا اور گلوکوما ہو گا۔

o- Oculomotor پلکوں کی حرکت سے متعلق ہے۔

o ٹروکلر- یہ پیگ آنکھ کے پٹھوں کے ساتھ کام کرتا ہے۔

o Trigeminal nerve brain peg کی خرابی چبانے اور پٹھوں کے اضطراب کا باعث بنتی ہے۔

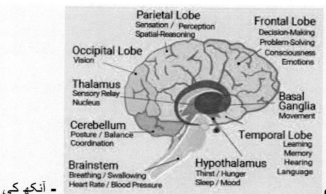

o **Abducens** - آنکھ کی

حرکت

o چہرے کے دماغ کے پگس - چہرے کی نقل و حرکت کا خدشہ ہے اور

چہرے کی رطوبتوں میں کمی آتی ہے اور ایک شخص چہرے کی سنسنابٹ

محسوس نہیں کرسکتا۔

o ویسٹیبلوکوکلیئر یا صوتی اعصاب - دماغی پیگ کی خرابی توازن یا حرکت

میں کمی کا باعث بنے گی۔

o اس دماغی پیگ کی گلوسوفرینج کی خرابی نگلنے اور سالویہ حاصل کرنے

میں دشواری کا باعث بنے گی کیونکہ نگلنے کے لیے خواہش کی ضرورت

ہوتی ہے۔

o **Vagus Loube**- یہ اعصاب فوبیا، تقریر، سانس، ہاضمہ اور اضطراری

سے متعلق ہے۔

o حتمی لوازمات - ایک دماغی پیگ ہے۔

o **Hypoglossal**- دماغ کا ایک اور پیگ ہے۔

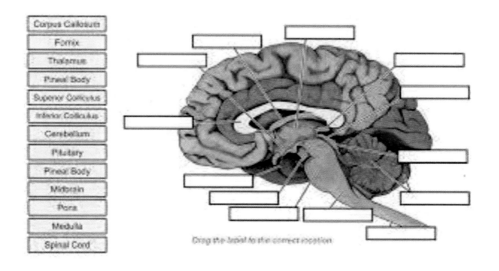

Corpus Callosum
Fornix
Thalamus
Pineal Body
Superior Colliculus
Inferior Colliculus
Cerebellum
Pituitary
Pineal Body
Midbrain
Pons
Medula
Spinal Cord

Drag the label to the correct location

There are 26 vertebrates in our Spine. The intervertebral disk is to protect the spinal cord. This disk is also known as a shock absorber for our spinal column. Each human spine has 24 ribs; these ribs are paired. There are 12 ribs on

each side of the spine resulting in 24 ribs in

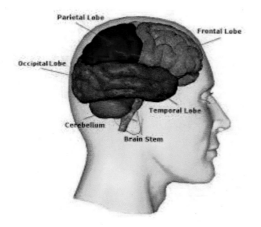

Parietal Lobe

Frontal Lobe

Occipital Lobe

Temporal Lobe

Cerebellum

Brain Stem

total. We do not consider the five ribs beneath

as true ribs in science but false, and the two

final pairs are considered as floating ribs. The

function of human ribs is to protect human vital

organs in the abdominal cavity, like our heart,

kidneys, spleen, etc...

The next major part of our skeleton is the

appendicular skeleton. The appendicular

skeleton forms the extremities of the body, such

as the arms, legs, pelvic, shoulder girdle and more. The shoulder girdle has 3 bones, which are the humorous, radius and the ulna. In the hand the wrist is called the carpal which is made of 8 bones and the metacarpals which have 5 bones, as well as 14 phalanges. The leg bones are connected to the pelvic girdle and the girdle has to coxal also known as hip bones. The human hip bone is made up of three bones, known as: the ilium, synthesis and the pubis. Leg bones are attached to the acetabulum. The bones in the legs are the femur, the tibia and the fibula. The proximal leg is attached to the tarsals which are composed of 7 bones. The Tarsals are connected to the 5 metatarsal bones in the foot; and, the metatarsals are connected to the 14 phalange bones. Our toes are known as phalanges. The calcaneus bone is also known as our heel. It's the heel of the foot.

ہماری ریڑھ کی ہڈی میں 26 فقرے ہیں۔ انٹرورٹیبرل ڈسک ریڑھ کی ہڈی کی

حفاظت کے لیے ہے۔ اس ڈسک کو ہمارے ریڑھ کی ہڈی کے کالم کے لیے

جھٹکا جذب کرنے والا بھی کہا جاتا ہے۔ ہر انسانی ریڑھ کی ہڈی میں 24

پسلیاں ہوتی ہیں یہ پسلیاں جوڑی جاتی ہیں۔ ریڑھ کی ہڈی کے ہر طرف 12

پسلیاں ہوتی ہیں جس کے نتیجے میں کل 24 پسلیاں ہوتی ہیں۔ ہم سائنس میں

نیچے کی پانچ پسلیوں کو حقیقی پسلیاں نہیں مانتے بلکہ جھوٹے ہیں، اور دو

آخری جوڑے کو تیرتی پسلیاں تصور کیا جاتا ہے۔ انسانی پسلیوں کا کام پیٹ کی

گہا میں انسانی اہم اعضاء کی حفاظت کرنا ہے، جیسے ہمارا دل، گردے، تلی

وغیرہ۔

ہمارے کنکال کا اگلا بڑا حصہ اپینڈیکولر کنکال ہے۔ اپینڈیکولر کنکال جسم کے

اعضاء کو تشکیل دیتا ہے، جیسے بازو، ٹانگیں، شرونی، کندھے کی کمر اور

بہت کچھ۔ کندھے کی کمر میں 3 ہڈیاں ہوتی ہیں جو کہ مزاحیہ، ریڈاس اور النا

ہیں۔ ہاتھ میں کلائی کو کارپل کہا جاتا ہے جو 8 ہڈیوں سے بنی ہوتی ہے اور

میٹا کارپل جس میں 5 ہڈیاں ہوتی ہیں، نیز 14 phalanges۔ ٹانگوں کی

ہڈیاں شرونیی کمر سے جڑی ہوتی ہیں اور کمر کو کوکسل کرنا ہوتا ہے جسے

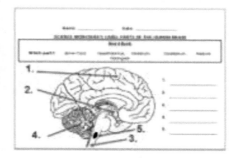

کولہے کی ہڈیاں بھی کہا جاتا ہے۔ انسانی کولہے کی ہڈی تین ہڈیوں سے مل کر

بنتی ہے، جنہیں کہا جاتا ہے: **ilium، synthesis** اور **pubis**۔ ٹانگوں

کی ہڈیاں ایسیٹابولم سے جڑی ہوتی ہیں۔ ٹانگوں میں ہڈیاں فیمر، ٹیبیا اور فیبولا

ہیں۔ قربت کی ٹانگ ٹارسل سے منسلک ہوتی ہے جو **7** ہڈیوں پر مشتمل ہوتی

ہے۔ ٹارسل پاؤں میں **5** میٹاٹرسل ہڈیوں سے جڑے ہوئے ہیں۔ اور،

metatarsals 14 phalange ہڈیوں سے جڑے ہوئے ہیں۔ ہماری

انگلیوں کو **phalanges** کے نام سے جانا جاتا ہے۔ کیلکنیئس ہڈی کو ہماری

ایڑی کے نام سے بھی جانا جاتا ہے۔ یہ پاؤں کی ایڑی ہے۔

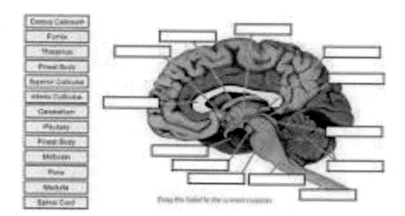

Drag the label to the correct position

Anatomy Quiz

Anatomy Test I I 1 اناٹومی ٹیسٹ **. What is the name of the distal bones of the leg between the patella and the tarsals** ڈسٹل ٹانگیک درمیان ےک ےس ٹارسل اور پٹیال ؟ےہ بڈیونکا نام کیا

_____

_____

2. What is the name of the largest bone of the body جسمیک سب ےس بڑی بڈیکا نامکیا ؟ےہ

_____

3. Which leg accounts for 1/3 of a humans height بن ۔ **1/3** اونچائیکا انسانیک ٹانگ یس کون ےہ ےت ی

_____

4. Which bone is connected distal to the tarsal ی ہوئ جڑی ےس دورےس ےس ٹارسل بڈی یس کون ۔ہے

_____

5. How many Kidneys should the human body have ی انسائ ی منیکتن جسم ہون گردے ی چاہئنی؟

_____

6. Where is the kidney located واقع کہاں گردہ ۔ےے

7 _____. How many bones are in the Skull منیکت کھوپڑی ۔ہنی ہڈیاں یت

_____

8. How many bones are in the Cranium ۔ہنی ہڈیاں یت

کرینیم منیکت _____

9. Name the Bones in the Cranium (8 points)
کرینیم منی ہڈیونکا نام بتائنی)8 پوائنٹس)

_____

_____

_____

_____

_____

_____

_____

_____

**10. Name 2 diseases that effect the Ears, Nose
and Throat (2 points)** کان، جو بتائنی نام کے بیماریوں ی 2 (ہنی
(پوائنٹس 2 کرئ متاثر کو ل گے اور ناک

_____

_____

_____

_____

_____

_____

**11. How many bones are in the fingers and
toes**_____ ہڈیاں یت
کت منیک انگلیوں اور انگلیوں ۔ہنی

12 _____ **. What
are brain cells?** دماغ ی ہنی؟ خلیات کیا

_____

_____

_____

_____

_____

_____

_____

_____

13. What juices are recommended for treating

Kidney disease (upto 3 points) ہنی) نن جاتی ننکون ےس

جوس تجویزک گردےیک بیماری ےک عالج ےک ل **3** (پوائنٹس تک

_____

_____

_____

14. How often should one use the restroom? یت ؟

بار بیت الخلاء استعمالکرنا چاہئ ی کت

_____

15. What is the cause of Heart attacks (upto 4

points) (ارٹ اٹیکیک وجہ کیا **4** پوائنٹس تک ہے ہ)

_____

_____

_____

_____

_____

_____

_____

16. Why are fingers and toes similar in science

or what similarities do they hold. سائنس منی انگلیاں اور

انگلیاں ایک جییسکیوں ہنی یا ان منیکیا ہے۔ جائ ی مماثلت پائ ی

_____

_____

17. What is the Scientific name for our wrist? ؟ہے

ہماری کلائی کا سائنس نام کیا ی

---

18. What is the Scientific name for our upper bone in our arm above the funny bone called? ہڈی

کیا ؟ہے ینی خنی مضحکہ نام سائنس ہڈیکا اوپری بازویک ہمارے اوپر کے

---

19. What is the section called between the wrist and the fingers in science? انگلیوں اور منی سائنس ی ؟ہنی ئ

ی کالئ کیاکہ صکو ہے لے وا درمیان کے

---

20. How many phalanges do we have including the distal, proximal and medial in the hands and the toes منی انگلیوں اور ہاتھ منی جن ہنی **phalanges** ہمارے

ہنی۔ شامل ی پاسکتن **medial** اور **proximal** ڈسٹل،

_____

_____

21. How many bones are in human hands and

feet? **کتنی ہڈیاں ہوتی ہیں انسان کے ہاتھ پاؤں میں؟**

_____

22. Explain ENT? (2 points) (2 پوائنٹس) کی وضاحت کریں؟

ENT

_____

_____

_____

_____

_____

_____

_____

23. Explain what are Kidney stones کہ وضاحت کرینک

گردے کی پتھری کیا ہنی؟

_____

_____

_____

_____

_____

_____

24. Explain one of the best teachings that you learned from one of our interns (upto 10 points) ن

ے س ہمارےکیس انی ر ین تعلیمیک وضاحتکریں جو آپ تی ایک بھی ی (سیکیھ
(ے ہ 10 پوائنٹس تک

_____

_____

_____

_____

_____

_____

Essay: Why is Proper Diet and Drinking the Proper Amounts of Water Beneficial to Our Health and Well Being? (Please explain in 2 Paragraphs for 15 points)

مضمون: مناسب خوراک اور پائ ی ہے؟)براہ کرم ننکیوں فائدہ مند نن اور یک مناسب مقدار پینا ہماری صحت

تندرسیت ےک ل 15 پوائنٹس ےک ل (2 پنیاگراف منی وضاحتکریں

_____

_____

_____

_____

_____

_____

_____

_____

_____

_____

_____

_____

Chapter III: Lesson III

Stroke and ENT

When the blood stops flowing, and then the person starts having a stroke, we could tell that the person is experiencing a stroke or has had a stroke by these acronyms. The acronyms are F. A. S. T. Which "F" is for facial drooping, "A" is for arm weakness, "S" is for speech difficulty, and "T" is for time. These acronyms help us to remember how we could see if a person is having a stroke.

First check to see if a person can smile. If they could smile then we know they're not having this joke. But when a person cannot smile there is a problem. There was one person, for example, that I met the other day who had a stroke. Sadly on one side of his face he could move, but the other side could not move. He tried to smile on one side of his face, and he could not close his eyes on the other side of his face. I am praying that God will heal him. His face was frozen on one side; however, on the other side he was able to move. I am praying that he would get healed.   The next observation is checking for weakness. If a person, or a patient comes in, and can not stretch their arms they may be having a stroke.

جب خون بہنا بند ہو جاتا ہے، اور پھر اس شخص کو فالج کا حملہ شروع ہو جاتا ہے، تو ہم بتا سکتے ہیں کہ اس شخص کو F. A. S. T فالج کا سامنا ہے یا اسے فالج ہوا ہے۔ مخففات بازو کی "A" ،چہرے کے جھکنے کے لیے ہے "F" ہیں۔ جو بولنے میں دشواری کے لیے ہے، "S" ،کمزوری کے لیے ہے

وقت کے لیے ہے۔ یہ مخففات ہمیں یہ یاد رکھنے میں "T" اور مدد کرتے ہیں کہ ہم کیسے دیکھ سکتے ہیں کہ آیا کسی شخص کو فالج کا حملہ ہے۔

پہلے چیک کریں کہ آیا کوئی شخص مسکرا سکتا ہے۔ اگر وہ مسکرا سکتے ہیں تو ہم جانتے ہیں کہ وہ یہ مذاق نہیں کر رہے ہیں۔ لیکن جب کوئی شخص مسکرا نہیں سکتا تو ایک مسئلہ ہوتا ہے۔ ایک شخص تھا، مثال کے طور پر، میں دوسرے دن ملا جس کو فالج کا دورہ پڑا تھا۔ افسوس سے اس کے چہرے کے ایک طرف وہ حرکت کر سکتا تھا، لیکن دوسری طرف ہل نہیں سکتا تھا۔ اس نے اپنے چہرے کے ایک طرف مسکرانے کی کوشش کی، اور وہ اپنے چہرے کے دوسری طرف آنکھیں بند نہ کر سکا۔ میں دعا کر رہا ہوں کہ خدا اسے شفا دے۔ اس کا چہرہ ایک طرف منجمد تھا۔ تاہم، دوسری طرف وہ منتقل کرنے کے قابل تھا۔ میری دعا ہے کہ وہ صحت یاب ہو جائے۔ اگلا مشاہدہ کمزوری کی جانچ کر رہا ہے۔ اگر کوئی شخص، یا کوئی مریض اندر آتا ہے، اور اپنے بازو نہیں پھیلا سکتا تو اسے فالج کا حملہ ہو سکتا ہے۔

When a person is experiencing a stroke they also have speech difficulty. If they can not say a funny sentence it may be a sign that they are experiencing a stroke. Things like that show that they had a stroke. It is helpful to watch for how long they're down, because there is medication that could reverse or slow down the brain damage.

So it's good to tell the doctor if the person was down for 30 or 20 min to help slow down the brain damage through medication. Another acronym is ENT which represents: Ears, Nose and Throat.

Diseases like ringing in the ears are diagnosed through an ENT specialist. Tinnitus is a disease that manifests when there is water in the ear. Tinnitus also causes dizziness.

This occurs when someone is taking a shower, the water goes in the ear, and it causes them to suffer with Tinnitus.

لہذا ڈاکٹر کو بتانا اچھا ہے کہ آیا وہ شخص 30 یا 20 منٹ کے لیے نیچے تھا تاکہ ادویات کے ذریعے دماغی نقصان کو کم کرنے میں مدد ہے جس کی نمائندگی کرتا ہے: ENT مل سکے۔ ایک اور مخفف کان، ناک اور گلا۔ کانوں میں گھنٹی بجنے جیسی بیماریوں کی ماہر کے ذریعے کی جاتی ہے۔ ٹنیٹس ایک بیماری ہے ENT تشخیص جو کان میں پانی آنے پر ظاہر ہوتی ہے۔ ٹنائٹس بھی چکر آنے کا سبب بنتا ہے۔

یہ اس وقت ہوتا ہے جب کوئی شخص نہا رہا ہوتا ہے، پانی کان میں جاتا ہے، اور اس کی وجہ سے انہیں **Tinnitus** کا سامنا کرنا پڑتا ہے۔

Racheal Ayeni- Nurse Volunteer

The Brain Stem and 3 Parts of the Brain.

The brian controls duties such as respiration. The brain is complex and it controls our memory and our emotions, vision, breathing and more...

The brain is composed of the cerebrum and the brains stem; and, the brain has 3 main parts. The cerebrum is the largest part of the brain. The brain interprets our vision, our hearing, our speech, our sense of reasoning emotions, learning even our fine control of movements (motor skills).

The cerebellum is located on the cerebrum, and it's function is to coordinate the motor movements and it maintains the posture and the balance.

The brain team operates as a relay center and connects the cerebellum and the cerebrum to the final work it performs

It performs the autonomic priority automatic function, such as breathing, body temperature, waking us up, digestion, sneezing, coughing and swallowing.

راحیل عینی۔ نرس رضاکار کے تنوں پر مشتمل ہوتا ہے۔ اور، دماغ کے **3** اہم حصے ہیں۔ سیریبرم دماغ کا سب سے بڑا حصہ ہے۔ دماغ ہماری بصارت، ہماری سماعت، ہماری تقریر، ہمارے استدلال کے جذبات کی ترجمانی کرتا ہے، یہاں تک کہ ہماری حرکات پر ٹھیک کنٹرول (موٹر سکلز) کو بھی سیکھتا ہے۔

سیریبیلم دماغی دماغ پر واقع ہے، اور اس کا کام موٹر کی نقل و حرکت کو مربوط کرنا ہے اور یہ کرنسی اور توازن کو برقرار رکھتا ہے۔

دماغی ٹیم ایک ریلے سینٹر کے طور پر کام کرتی ہے اور دماغی اور دماغی دماغ کو اس آخری کام سے جوڑتی ہے جسے وہ انجام دیتا ہے۔

یہ خود مختار ترجیحی خودکار کام انجام دیتا ہے، جیسے سانس لینا،

جسم کا درجہ حرارت، ہمیں جگانا، ہاضمہ، چھینکنا، کھانسی اور

نگلنا۔

Conclusion

First graders and students you are learning like little bees! Remember your Anatomy!! This information will be helpful in your future as you continue to grow and learn more and more about the structure of the human body. The next part of this book will give thanks to our Nurses and credits where credits are due. Continue to strive and prepare for your next text book in the Second Grade!!

Thank you to our Nurse Interns for Anatomy and Physiology Part I for 1st Graders

Racheal Ayeni- Nurse Volunteer

Thank you to our Nurse Interns for Anatomy and

Physiology Part I for 1st Graders

Ms. Elise- Nurse

Thank you to our Nurse Interns for Anatomy and Physiology Part I for 1st Graders

Ms. Sylvia- Nurse

Works Cited:

These notes were compiled in class lectures

and with our Interns that are Volunteer nurses.

Word & Biography From Dr. Tasha Taylor

God bless you and succeed because I love you,

Dr. Tasha Taylor was born in September

to Brother Anthony Taylor and Apostle Sandra

Mitchell. Dr. Tasha Taylor is the oldest of 12

brothers and sisters and has 1 biological son

Joshua Josma and several Spiritual sons and daughters which some are listed below with the names of their Churches, Outreach Ministries and /or Schools. Dr. Taylor is the founder of, "Reaping Time Outreach Worship Center." Reaping Time Outreach Worship Center supports and/ or covers over 20 Churches, Outreach Ministries, Schools and Orphanages.

A. Reaping Time Outreach Faith Mission Kenya with Boniface Obando Okwiri

B. Women With A Call International Founder Apostle Dr. Elizabeth Hairston-McBurrows

C. Agape Pentecostal Church of Pakistan with Pastor Pervez Patrus

D. Paradise Orphanage with Pastor Pervez Patras Pervaiz

E. Music School - Pastorsania Pastorsania

F. Tasha Taylor Christian School, High School and Seminary with Pastor Pervez Patrus

G. Reaping Time Outreach Worship Kenya Ministry with Pastor Nyaruri Pastor Mandere Richard

H. Beloved Princess Orphanage with Pastor Moses Owiti

I. Reaping Time Outreach Pakistan Ministry with Pastor Sharjeel Gill

J. Light of Hope Orphanage Pastor Sharjeel Gill

K. Jesus Christ Sunday School - Evangelist Amber

L. Grace Pentecostal Church of India Pastor Emmanuel

Emmanuel

M. Reaping Time Outreach Worship Centers I with

Bishop Martin Wachira

N. Reaping Time Outreach Worship Center II with

Bishop Martin Wachira

O. Reaping Time Outreach Worship Center III with

Bishop Martin Wachira

P. Reaping Time Outreach Worship Center IV with

Bishop Martin Wachira

Q. Reaping Time Outreach Worship Center V. With

Bishop Martin Wachira

V with Bishop Martin Wachira

N. Going the Extra Mile to Feed the Needy with Bishop

Martin Wachira

O. Rikambi Fellowship Church Church- Pastor Ptr Brian

Okemwa

P. Pastor Okemwa's Orphanage

Q. Holy Purpose Gospel Ministry of Pakistan with

Evangelist Shahid and Nagina Majid

R. Faith Revivals Ministry- Pastor Samuel Khokhar,

Pastor Sharif Khokhar, and Evangelist Nabila

Waqas

S. Global Youth Prayer Network- Pastor Samuel A.

Johnson

T. Children for Sunday School - Pastor Pastorsamuiel Javed

Dr. Tasha Taylor is also a Graduate of, "National School of Theology" under Founder, Dr. Orlando Short. Also, Dr. Tasha Taylor is covered by, "The Apostolic Prophetic Connection" under her Apostle, Dr. Elizabeth Hairston McBurrows and Elder Carlton McBurrows.

When attending class take very good notes:

_____

_____

_____

_____**The End.**

Made in the USA
Columbia, SC
22 May 2023

16603617R00058